LABYRINTH

INDIA · SINGAPORE · MALAYSIA

Notion Press

No.8, 3rd Cross Street,
CIT Colony, Mylapore,
Chennai, Tamil Nadu – 600004

First Published by Notion Press 2020
Copyright © Mustafa Mun 2020
All Rights Reserved.

ISBN 978-1-63633-537-7

LABYRINTH

Your Personal Handbook on Getting Through the Maze of Life

MUSTAFA MUN

INDIA • SINGAPORE • MALAYSIA

IND!CACADEMY

Indic Pledge

———◆◆———

- *I celebrate our civilisational identity, continuity & legacy in thought, word and deed.*

- *I believe our indigenous thought has solutions for the global challenges of health, happiness, peace and sustainability.*

- *I shall seek to preserve, protect and promote this heritage and in doing so,*
  - *discover, nurture and harness my potential,*
  - *connect, cooperate and collaborate with fellow seekers,*
  - *advance diversity and inclusivity in the society.*

About Indic Academy

———◆◆———

Indic Academy is a non-traditional 'university' for traditional knowledge. We seek to bring about a global renaissance based on Indic civilizational and indigenous thought. We are pursuing a multidimensional strategy across time, space and cause by establishing centers of excellence, transforming intellectuals and building an ecosystem.

Indic Academy is pleased to support this book.

"Thanks to everyone for their help in any form that inspired me to complete this work."

I dedicate this work to everyone who has made some noise in my life.

CONTENTS

PREFACE

It has taken me a while to complete this book. I am not targeting anyone; my target audience is undefined. All I believe is that whoever reads this book should end up with a free and open mind.

Labyrinth is a collection of thoughts – a piece of work designed to open the eyes of people who would wish to know the meaning of life and their existence.

I intend to pass on a message with this book, which people easily overlook. I dont want to target any religious group or philosophy as it may easily raise doubts in peoples minds about my intentions. It is only a glimpse of what life could be if we saw it from a 360° perspective, although many may find my views tedious and may resent it.

I never felt that *Labyrinth* would be published. But I wanted to make sure that at least a few people should read it if it does. I want my readers to understand what I am trying to say and pass the message to others.

Nothing said in this world is left in vain, or no action is left undone. Everything has a purpose, and the purpose has to be fulfilled. *Labyrinth* has its purpose: the purpose of making a purpose. I hope you realize its purpose.

REALIZATION

Humans generally do not care for what they have than what they dont. They usually believe in achieving the ultimate desire of their choice. They submit their mind and energy concentrated on the fact that they are going to get it someday. When they achieve that, they lose everything that they had and run for attaining that back.

This happens with every person—be it be a spiritually enlightened person or a layman—and it has always continued over the years and maybe will continue forever. Dynasties have disappeared for this human urge and many have risen to power.

I am saying this because I have also suffered from this urge. This was due to a desire that I always had. Our mind is an extraordinary and powerful organ that has the capability to achieve almost anything it wants to achieve. It can make you a billionaire if you really want, or you can end up becoming broke with the same mind as yours. Still, it is also true that it is as soft as clay and from birth, it starts moulding itself in the way others mend it.

Back at home, I always thought that I was in a prison of some sort and was held captive with everyone trying to check every single move and making things a bit uncomfortable. But as every child, I went through that phase naturally until I made a choice, a choice to achieve something more, for which I had to leave the family.

I decided to study overseas for my further education, and it would turn out to be a long time for me. A person who had never stepped out alone in his own country had to personally undergo mentally rigourous training to acclimatize to the new surroundings. When I reached the place of my dreams, I realized that sometimes we expect something to happen early, and it turns out to be too early for us to discover the truth of life.

It was a long time from the time of my applications till the time I reached the airport. Yet, my thoughts kept killing me and haunting me with the fact that I was alone. It is contradictory and ironic for me to say such a thing, as back home, I was pleading to be released out of the so-called prison, and when I was, I realized that freedom was not that free.

Freedom comes with a price that one needs to pay. I paid that and with interest, too. I loved my home but never expressed my love. Whereas my family loved me so much that they did not want me out of their sight. Their love for me is still beyond bounds, but as I said before, humans do not value the things around them. I did care, but when I realized that I was doing injustice to myself by staying in a shell and by being like a bird in a cage, I decided to make a change in life.

Yeah, life, well, whatever you call it, is the weirdest of the weird mysteries that one can unfold. I have still not understood life very well, but so far, its been a very good learning experience for me. I have faced difficulties that I have had to overcome. Difficulties which I saw as difficult but which many may find a piece of cake. Well, they were what I called a "learning experience".

I got done with school and college, and during all those twelve-fourteen years of education, every time I saw a beautiful picture of an overseas institute, I would imagine myself studying out there and making my parents proud. It came with a huge price, though, but I was willing to pay it. More than my parents, I underwent severe mental training to go and study in an overseas university. The moment I landed there I thought, *what have I done? Am I prepared for whats going to come now?* Such questions kept going around my brain like a rollercoaster, but I was unable to find the answer.

I soon entered my room, kept my bags inside, emptied my bags out, and with every piece of shirt I took out, I remembered the person who packed the bag with love and care. I emptied my whole luggage and soon got settled. I immediately gave a missed call back home and realized that it was too early for that. I heard my mothers voice heavy with sleep, but as soon as she heard my voice, she was as fresh as a young child and spoke with me as if she hadnt heard from me in ages.

I was in an unstable frame of mind and realized that there were too many things I was missing back at home. At home, I did get all that I wanted except the one thing that I got when I came here: myself. Yes, people do realize who they are or where they stand once they are put into the shoes of reality and faced with the strife and hardships of daily life. I realized the same when I came to this place that life has much more to offer than what we see. Its not just the materialistic world but also the importance of opening ones vision; it may happen in many ways, and it happened to me on that day.

It is weird, you see, that we often say that time is really bad, but time moves on, and you are never in the same time frame as before. It just slips away, and even before you realize, hours and months pass by, sometimes even years, and you are left in awe, frustration, and disaster. If its karma, and people say, "Youll see, what goes around comes back round to you," it is bullshit. I believe in something more. The fact of reality, the fact of understanding the nature of time and not karma, because karma is not dependent on time. But if we hold them both together and integrate them to form a third force equivalent to the spiritual force thats called faith, I guess thats when we get the answers to our questions. People generally expect—and the expectations never end—and dream of having a new car, a new phone, a new girlfriend, etc., but shit happens.

I often used to fight with my loved ones back at home; my grandmother and I used to fight over small things; my friends and I never had a day where I hadnt fought with someone. Things were just too loud. My locality had people screaming downstairs and drunk people went up and down the street yelling at the top of their voices. I regretted being there. My mom always came in to ask me how I was, and

I used to shrug her off. There was never a time when I did not think, *why the hell am I trapped in this shit hole?* But now, at times, I regret that. Not those shouts and screams on the road or those fights I had with my grandmother and my friends. I miss something even more special — the touch of my mothers hand. I kind of miss it too much nowadays. People think I am being sarcastic when I say this, but it is true. Sometimes you are just disappointed with being someone you dont want to be, but you regret it in the future.

The future is not written. There is no fate but what we make for ourselves. If this is true, I just wrote something of which I am still surprised. I just wish I could believe that from the time I wake up till the time I put my head on the same bed and pillow.

Yet I didnt get any sleep even in the quietest environment until I realized that what I looked at wasnt what I saw. They were just beliefs or thoughts that I carried around with me, which had created its world. I started to think those thoughts had started to meddle with my mind, going deeper and deeper, analyzing every move that I made. I started to realize that whatever I thought and believed made a huge impact on what I perceived, and that is how it exactly worked. For a second, I just sat on the bed, looked at my watch, saw it closer and closer and heard the seconds pass. Then I realized that I was being a fool. I should just give up what I believe in and trust what I want to see and I saw what I wanted to see. I saw something that every man dreams of when he feels that he wants to be rescued from the clutches of time and the duality of fate. I saw a hand come out to me and grab my hand, and I was thrown back, far away, back to where I stood, in the same place, doing the same thing but differently.

Do you ever think what your purpose in life is? Are you just here to work, sleep, eat and live life day to day and just hoping that youre still breathing the next day? Lately, Ive been looking into my life from different perspectives. Not sure if Im having an early mid-life crisis or whether I have been struck by a bolt, but Ive been feeling like I dont give enough back and need to get more involved in more important topics other than what brand of laptop one is using or what make of mobile someone has. I feel so guilty for living in this luxury even though my luxury is only a two-bedroom apartment in Mumbai. But now, I have ended up all alone in these residential halls, which still is en suite, and I thank myself for receiving such forms of luxury.

I feel that I need to make a difference and have a purpose of serving while Im here in this world. If I can lend a helping hand to making someones life better, or get more involved in world economics, then I would feel more fulfilled. Something is missing in me, and I think I found it but have not yet found a way to trigger that inner voice in me. Maybe its because I dont know the path I need to walk on, or maybe its because I need a helping hand to show me the road to becoming more active. All I know is I dont want to live a life trying to make ends meet and worrying about topics that are small compared to human starvation and the corrupt politics in third-world countries. I want to leave this world with an impact, not just as a lost soul without a cause.

A HAMMER AND A MAN

If you imagine a hammer that does nothing and lies in a box all day long, you will not feel anything for it. Its just a hammer, and it does not have a soul or any feelings. Now imagine the same hammer with a soul. Just like a person, that hammer too feels now. He stays in a box, not knowing why he feels what he feels. He feels strange lying in the toolbox all day but does not know why that is so. He considers if something is missing in his life. But if that was true, he does not know what that missing thing is.

One day, a person snatches the hammer from the toolbox and breaks some branches with it. It was a new experience for the hammer. He was happy. He was happy being held, wielded and hit on the branch. The hammer loved everything about that experience. But when he was again in the toolbox, he felt something missing. He was unsatisfied with what he did that day. He felt happy but still unsatisfied.

After that one day, the hammer was used frequently. He was used to hit some rocks, he was used to fix the table leg and so on. But he still felt something was missing. He thought he probably has not done as much as he should have. Maybe he needed to be used more to feel satisfied.

But then, someday, someone used the hammer on a nail and just then, the hammer felt utter satisfaction. His soul was satisfied and he understood what it is that he was designed to do. The nails were what was missing from his life. And now his soul felt fulfilled because he was finally doing what he ought to do.

Humans are just like a hammer. They do not know what is missing from their lives and what will end that emptiness from their lives. Even in a Nazi prison, Corri ten Boom was fully satisfied with god. We are the ones who find our satisfaction. We can have faith in a rock thinking its god and can still be satisfied.

Sometimes you meet people who seem alive from the inside when you look at them. They care about their work, they care about the people around them and they care for the people they work for. Their joy is not artificial. It is coming from the inside. While looking at them, you feel their trueness and know that they are truly happy.

When you see these people, you look at them and say they are happy because they know what they are doing and where it will take them. They know why they are here and how they will change the world. This quality of theirs makes them stand out in the crowd where most of us stay hidden. Are you someone who would like to feel the same satisfaction they feel?

Now imagine that you are building a house and you have hired a contractor. Imagine that the contractor does not go according to the blueprints designed by your architect and starts working without a plan. As absurd as it sounds, it will not work because the contractor needs to know where to put the walls and windows. Otherwise, the house will look entirely different from what you want it to look like. At that moment you only wish that the architect works with the contractor in good terms and is clear about his blueprints with him. But this does not always happen. If the architect is your friend or family, he will be willing to go an extra mile for you, but in other cases, you might need to pay him more. The thing is, like an architect, you cannot bribe life.

In these events of events passing by, my mind started becoming more analytical and acted more than a students; it was evolving. I did not know it but I could feel it. Maybe I was going mad, but the silence crept over me. I just could not bear it anymore. The kind of silence that I longed for was becoming a slow poison for me, its chemical chain reaction acting rapidly in just one manner. SILENCE. *Why are people so quiet over here until they are drunk?* I kept looking at them and saw that something was missing in them, something that they all longed for but most of them did not have in them and just made others believe that it existed in and around them, without any evidence. Paper walls were created which were thick enough to keep a thought from disturbing their artificial world of creation.

We are human beings and we all have an emotion of "self" inside us. This emotion makes us aware of our surroundings and ourselves. This is the reason why we understand our five senses and the view of the world which we have. It is different from that of others but we all have it. To us, the world is where things happen regularly. We mend in the way our surroundings and culture mend us. Even though we are highly affected by our surroundings, we do have our perspective toward things. And this is the reason why we think that all of us are important and are here for a good reason no matter what the situation is. If we look at the logic behind our existence, we will see that there will be no changes in the world after our deaths; it will go on as it is now. Only our friends and family members will remember us. But we ignore this logic because it does not suit the idea of existence as a great deal and improvement in the world. We willingly let go of the fact that we have no such importance in this world and humanity as a whole will not be affected by our being or not being.

If we hold on to the belief that we are important in this world, it is safe to assume that we are here in this world for a purpose and sometimes it is not what we think it is. This purpose is not as small as taking care of a family member or being nice to others. The purpose is grander than it seems.

Whenever I meet someone new and create a bond with them, I always think that they will at least say hi when we meet again, but always in vain. That never happens. When you find them sitting somewhere, they do not even look up to see who it is. They go on with their work taking no notice of the person standing behind them. They behave as if the person never existed. This puzzle gets harder to solve every time I meet someone new.

If we apply logic to the question of existence or life and if we are here for a reason, we have to conclude that our existence must be necessary for some purpose or the other, whether big or small, otherwise, we would not exist. This satisfies our need to feel important about our existence. Because we do not know what we are here for and what is required for us to do. In the end, when the time comes, we would have done our deed without knowing that we have. We have fulfilled the purpose. In the short term, what we do and what we choose not to do are all part of a plan. No matter what happens, the plan will always be there being fulfilled. You do not know what that plan is, but you only believe that there is one.

If we are living our lives without thinking about a plan, we will go on living without being worried about the plan. We will think that our actions are free and we are living by free will. But if it is a part of a greater plan, then are we free?

THE PLAN

There can be other ways to look at the greater plan for human beings, the reason for our existence and the reason why our existence matters. What is the great goal of human existence? Instead of looking at the reason for only one persons existence, we can try looking at humanitys reason for existence. Then probably the existence of an individual or their actions is not much important for the plan.

Lets take a little help from science to understand the meaning of existence. Consider billions of electrons that are going to the path of least resistance. They reach a gate that allows 30% to go left and 70% to go right. The gate stands there to let electrons pass but that gate cannot decide which electrons will go right and which will go to the left. It can neither stop an electron nor let it pass on its records. The gate only decides the percentage.

Just like electrons, we are following our paths too without knowing that we are a part of a great circuit and in the end, it will generate power. As individuals, those electrons know nothing about their destiny; they do not know if there is any plan bigger than following the circuit board. This way neither electrons nor we have a choice to get away from the circuit board. It does not matter which electrons take what route to reach the destination, it will not affect the outcome. It is a fact that those electrons choose their route. But it still is unimportant. The important part is that they make other devices work. Are we like these electrons too? Is it possible that we do not have any signs like those electrons? Is it possible that as individual humans, we have no value, but as a collective, we are of greater importance?

To look at it holistically, try to see the universe as a whole and the elements it contains. Everything that exists in the universe is due to the big bang. Some things are made of the same elements, only they contain different amounts of different things. The human race, too, is made of photons and is a part of the galaxy. And it is made of the same elements as any other thing. When you will look at the stars, again you will eventually feel the same. Because now you know that you too are made of stardust and you are a part of the universe. No matter how small you think your existence means, the galaxys outcome was you and it cannot be for no reason. Maybe the real question is: why does the galaxy exist?

Throughout generations, we have read about people who suffered and died for the wellbeing of others. They did not know if this was the reason for their existence but still, they made it a reason and sacrificed themselves for a cause. Maybe when they were dying they felt satisfied thinking that they did something good for humanity. Some would have thought that this was the only reason why they ever existed. Some of those people knew that that was what they required to do and god directed them towards it. Maybe they were right, maybe people who still think that are right, but what was achieved? A good life for those who got left? What does a more comfortable life mean to people who were going to live anyway? Living more comfortably does not affect the greater plan, if there is any. Life and we go on as those electrons, no matter what situation we live in.

OUR PURPOSE

What is the real question behind why we exist? Why do we search for the significance and objective of our being? When we think of what we are here for, what is the real question that we are asking?

What does existence mean? We see an object that is observable and believes that it exists. Other objects exist but they are not visible to the naked eye and do not take a shape or form a structure. If there are things that humans claim that they exist, they should be visible and observable, otherwise, that object does not exist. These things that cannot be observed might exist in another universe and another space, but here, if it does not have a structure to show which affects humans in one way or another, it does not exist. If one thing is not visible, observable and does not affect anything, then its existence can be disregarded.

Humans exist and they have a lot of things to show their existence. They can be seen on a large scale; they are observable both physically and psychologically. Scientifically too they have a structure that can be seen by other human beings and lively objects. Humans do exist!

When the question of our existence is clear, now we might think why we exist. Do we have a purpose or were we only created by some events of chemicals that happened with time? Do we have an assigned purpose?

Tell me one thing: why does it matter so much to find a purpose? What does it matter if there is an objective to our existence or not?

You do so many things that have no context to them at all. Lets say you have soup instead of vegetables for dinner. It will not make a difference and is not a part of a greater plan. But when you suddenly know that having soup has a purpose behind it, then it suddenly becomes important. Similarly, if you are making an app based on a website, then making that website has a plan behind it and the first part of the plan will be completed when you make that website.

Small projects matter when they are a part of a large project. Then completing one project means that one step of the large project is done. If you are not happy with your financial status, you will work on getting more money. Getting a new job that pays more than the last one will be the first step and you will feel satisfied knowing that job switching had a goal behind it. On the other hand, when you take a tool and dig a hole in your backyard without having a goal in mind, then digging that hole was pointless and it had no meaning or purpose.

To feel accomplished you dont need to take on hard goals. They can be small and simple projects which you achieve because they entertain you or give you happiness. But the human mind is complicated, it needs a big, complicated project to feel happy or accomplished. Digging a hole should be relevant if it gives you happiness but our mind will not listen.

Sometimes we confuse goals with projects and we keep working on them even though they have been achieved. Goals are where you want to be when you have completed the project. And projects are the actions that you take to reach the goal. Owning a house is the goal and making loan payments to own the house are projects.

So the first thing you need to do is set some goals and decide the projects. Divide those projects into small parts and complete them one by one. When all projects are done you will reach the goal.

Now lets think about why goals matter. If projects matter because they are important to reaching a goal, then the context for goal matters too. If your goal is to reach the end of the tunnel without a context to reach the end of the tunnel, then completing that project and achieving your goal is pointless because it has no context. A goal needs to have a context if it matters. If your goal is to increase your salary but you do not know why you need to have more money, it does not matter if you have more money. It will not make a difference just as eating soup instead of vegetables does not.

It is a human need to know what it is that matters. The need to know why we are here surviving, living a comfortable life. If any goal improves the way you live or complete your projects then it is important too. Connecting with other human beings is another need of humans. It does not come to us with time. It is there from birth.

If our goals are there only to complete our emotional and physical needs then the context of goals is survival. This way if we make more money it makes us feel more secure about the future. Looking for a partner and starting a life with them completes our need to socialize and feel connected to other people. In the same way, there are techniques to improve ourselves at other levels, like learning new skills to do better in career and taking a step ahead.

For a minute think if your goals have a greater meaning than only satisfying your physical or emotional needs. Now your whole life is upside down and you will be confused to make any decision. You will set goals that have nothing to do with your satisfaction.

Some will say that purpose might not be important to survive but it is a spiritual need. It is a nice way to look at the purpose but if it is not required for survival, it is not as useful as one thinks it is. So it can be put aside for a while now. Lets talk about the purpose that is something greater than just for emotional and physical needs.

If you only set your goals based on your need, then you will never set goals that go beyond your need. You will not do that because you see no context to them. Even if those goals are bigger than the goals you have achieved or are trying to achieve, you will not set them because those goals will not directly affect your life. Those who work on those goals are people like Gandhi and Mother Teresa. These people thought way beyond their personal needs and set some goals for themselves. They achieved them and became someone great. If you only achieved goals based on your needs, then you will never get closer to those people. You will aim to survive comfortably and this is how far you will go. All you hope for is a nice life, anything beyond that is not even imaginable by you.

Goals based on needs are complicated. When you have reached the point where all your needs are satisfied, you will still be setting the goals for need because you do not know that all your needs have been satisfied. When you have been doing it all your life it is hard to push yourself past this. Most of you might have reached this point long ago. Some of you are still going through the trouble of making goals and accomplishing them. I have reached that point and I believe I will be able to maintain this achievement for a long time. Now I do not see a point in setting up goals merely based on my needs. My only motivation for goals is to keep my living the way it is so that my life does not take a step back. My goals can motivate me to achieve something better, but this better is only the better version of the goals I have already achieved. These are not the goals that go beyond my need. There are goals that one can achieve that are great and interesting and does not fall under the category of need.

For some people, need-based goals let them achieve so much more than they set their goals for. For example, if one person is poor and they decide to become financially well to take care of their family, then they will set a goal. That goal can take them to become extremely wealthy. So their only goal proved to be the greater goal. Similarly, if one person has suffered from cancer, then they might start working on their health and achieve a greater goal. But there comes a point when needs dry out too and you have nothing to achieve anymore. You will know if that has happened to you. When you try to set some goals that do not have a greater context, you find them troubling and start thinking if they are worth it. Most of us hear the voice saying why bother? And this is the reason most people only earn +/−10% of their income throughout their lives. They did not set great goals and they did not meet them. Without goals, there will be no changes in anyones life.

So if you are stuck at this point in life, stop worrying about your needs anymore. Go beyond them. If you have already completed the small projects, then you can stop doing them again and again. They are not doing anything good in your life. They are only wasting your time. For example, if you have finished your dinner then there is no use of continuing stirring the sauce. Dinner is done, the project is done and the goal has been achieved.

So if you have reached the point where you are not getting anything from need-based goals, then you need to look for a context that is not based on your need. That new goal will push you to do something productive. People are stuck in this situation because they did not think of their goals. If you decided to double your income by the end of the year, you might feel discouraged because you had no context for why you want to double your income. Did you need more money? But you already have enough, so why? These are the goals that make you feel stuck because you get nowhere with them. This goal seemed more troubling than the actual gain, so you left it in the middle. You did not want to be bothered by it because it had no apparent context.

Another way of setting goals is the purpose. The purpose does not depend on need. Purpose can exist with need too. They can both work in your life simultaneously. You can set multiple goals with multiple projects in life and like that you can have multiple contexts too.

If you set your goals based on a purpose, you will realize that it is much more motivating then need-based goals. Purpose-based goals are interesting and they require more energy. Need only works under survival, but purpose has more context to it. It allows you to set goals that are way beyond your reach and keeps you motivated for them and when your projects are done, you finally reach those goals that seemed so far away before. You will find your purpose hidden in your talent and your passion. Passion lets you do great things and talent motivates you to do those great things. Purpose works well because it does not let your inner fire go out. When you have only need to worry about, then your inner fire is not that lit as it should be, because need is about survival and you are surviving anyway. But when you work with a purpose, you have a passion inside you, you have that fire that keeps saying go on and do not stop. When you start looking for a partner, if that is based only on need of not wanting to be alone forever, you might get discouraged because the context does not have passion. But when you look for a partner with passion, need and desperation, you will get success. The reason why you might not succeed while looking for a partner based on need is that when you get tired of looking for one you will get used to being alone. After some time, you will find yourself ok and not in want of a partner anymore. When you have a passion to find a partner, you will realize that you can attract suitable partners towards you because you are now looking for someone to share your energy with and not to stop feeling alone. Desperation drives people crazy and others get away from them, but with passion, everyone gets closer to you. Think of it this way. Imagine a partner and now imagine yourself with them. Which version would they like: the one that lives with passion or the one that lives for survival? If you managed to get a partner based on needful desire, then they will have the same context for a partner too. Your whole relationship will be based only on need instead of passion. If you find a mate with a purpose in mind, your relationship will be bigger than only need. You both can achieve greater and more exciting goals. When there are no needs in mind while setting a goal, the goal becomes so much more than just a goal. You are not only surviving, you are living to your potential. Your relationship will be formed based on something bigger than just need. It does not need to be a romantic relationship. Relationships can be of various kinds. You can be partners, you can be lovers, you can be friends, you can be whatever you want to be and set goals.

Purpose is better than need because it does not demotivate you when you have nothing to gain from it. When you are starving you fight to get food but when you are already full and doing better in life, your motivation to get food will be gone. You will not fight anymore. The more you complete your need-based goals, the weaker motivation gets to set new goals. You get no context to set new goals, and life gets boring without something interesting happening. Purpose makes you go on even when you have achieved one goal, it does not let you stop because the goal has not been achieved yet. It becomes more powerful as you keep working on it.

The third thing that passion brings in for you is discipline. In times of need, you are desperate to survive. But with a purpose, you have passion and talent waiting for you to flourish them. Your goals are there waiting for you to achieve them. It becomes easier to set new goals. You do not feel stuck anymore. Your goals will be interesting but easy and simple. They will not stress you out or make you feel depressed over them. They will make you happy and more energetic. For example, if your passion and talent lie in singing, you will not feel stressed because it is something you like. This is where your heart is at; you do not need to push yourself to like singing because you already love that. So when you set a goal and make small projects to reach it, you will feel motivated to do it every day. Not everyone is privileged enough to work with their passion. So most of us only work within our needs. This need makes us do things that we do not want to do, like working for a living or doing a bank job when our passion lies in painting. Eventually, your energy will drain out and you will want to quit. You will get tired of everything and everyone out there. You will only want peace but that peace will be hard to get. This happens when you have been doing need-based goals for a long time.

One more benefit of working within purpose context is that some of your need-based goals get fulfilled without even being set. The purpose is a powerful context that does wonderful things on its own. Think about some project you have done or is in line to be one. Sometimes one project does the work of other work too while being in progress. You can do this too, only you need to set the right goals. Those goals will not fulfil your need and also fuel the fire inside you. So if you love to paint and become a painter, you might get famous and become rich. This way, your need is fulfilled and your passion for painting stays there with you. You are now handling your needs with passion; you do not need to do the things you dislike or do not know how to do. Your needs and wants are satisfied using the passion and talent within you.

So it is pretty clear that it is important to know what your purpose is. Otherwise, you will always be stuck in the need-based context. It puts limitations on your life and your life becomes only a need to survive physically and emotionally. The goals that need a greater context will be out of your reach. Your motivation to set goals and fulfil them will become weaker with time. The more successful you get, the weaker your mindset will be at setting new goals for life. The best thing you can hope from life is to take time to achieve those goals to stay motivated. When goals are met, you live the same life every day again and again. This is a circle that you get tired of with time.

When you have a purpose in life, you feel stronger than before and feel powerful when you set new goals. Think of a life where you are doing small projects to reach a goal and those projects are not interesting. You are bad at those projects and it takes so much time to complete them. Think about how helpless you will feel not knowing what you are doing and if it has anything in it for you. Then suddenly its time for a new project which is interesting and full of energy. This new project makes you happy because you can improve your skills and enhance your talent. After a while, you will see that the second project does the job of the first project too. You see no point in doing the first project then. Now its time for you to decide which project you like.

The thing is, you dont need to become super talented in the field of need-based context to start setting goals on purpose-based context. Naturally, you cannot master the art of survival too, you just survive somehow. The better you survive, the weaker you get at achieving things. I am not asking you to start ignoring your needs; you can start setting goals based on need, only you need to put the second context in the back too: the context of purpose. This way your goals will not be only about survival.

What are those things that you can do under the context of purpose but cannot do under the context of need? You can start cooking and make a YouTube channel. You might not get anything from it but you will be satisfied because you love to cook and you can share your talent with someone. This will not be irrelevant and neither will it be pointless if it makes you happy.

If you do not know your purpose in life, it will not be a waste of time if you took some time off from work and tried to find it. It changes your life and how you feel about it. It is easy to turn need goals into passion goals: you only need to find your passion.

DEEPER FOCUS ON PURPOSE

The more I have researched it, the more I realized that everyone who has ever written about purpose thinks it is inbuilt in us and needs to be found by ourselves. When you read such books, you sit in a corner and think what drives you to set your goals and write it down. You think that it is your purpose. Sometimes it changes and you update it from time to time.

I think all of this is not true. Purpose is not inbuilt in us. Of course, if you are born to some great person, you will have some of their qualities. You will want to do great things too, but that does not mean that is your lifes purpose. In most cases, when you sit down and write down a statement of your purpose you will end up with something which does not make any sense. But you will work hard to make sense of it because you believe it is what you were looking for.

If you start working on a purpose based on that statement, you will end up getting stuck in the purpose and what it means. It will be a house of things that dont even matter. When you feel stuck and confused, you will wonder if you are just guessing to find your purpose. Most of the time, you will not be satisfied with what you have written. After a week or month, when you will look back at your notepad, you will see that those ideas were nothing but air and now they are not that interesting as they were before.

When I tried to do the same thing with a notepad, I felt that I was doing it wrong. How exactly are we supposed to find our purpose? How will we know if what we have written is right or not? Who will tell us? Should we write down everything we like to do and then decide which one we like best? Or do we just try harder and harder till we get only one answer? But what if we never get an answer?

But the truth is if you do not have a divine or genetic purpose it does not mean you do not have a purpose at all. A purpose is not something you get with birth. It is something that you create based on the reality you live in. Maybe it is not a free choice too, but you will have the freedom of choosing one thing over another based on what is more valid to you.

You only need to develop a technique using which you can get your purpose. There can be a process to get the result and you will trust that process too because you are the one who made it.

HOW TO INTELLIGENTLY DEFINE YOUR PURPOSE

I have come up with two techniques to know your purpose. You can use both if you like; they both help you figure out different aspects of purpose. You might find it hassling and a lot of work, but every second of it is worth it because after this, you will never feel stuck again. It will be easier for you to take action on your decision since there is clarity now.

Method 1: Emotional Intelligence

The purpose is highly derived from passion, so the first thing you need to do is get clear with your emotional intelligence. When you find your purpose, you will know that it is something that you are passionate about and your emotions will agree with what you have found.

But before trying out methods you need to be clear about your life. You need to figure out the context of your life. Only then you will be emotionally available for your purpose-hunting. Without knowing this, it will not work.

To use a method, first imagine you are trying to find a way to someplace. Lets say you are visiting India for the first time and trying to locate where Delhi is. If you have a map of India in your hands, you will probably find it in no time. You will look at the map and Delhi will be one of the highlighted cities that catches your eye as soon as you open the map. Within seconds, youll know where Delhi is. Lets imagine a scenario where you are looking at Indias map from the 1920s. You will still find Delhi there, but it will take you some time because that map will not be as detailed as todays map. You will also find it difficult to find a route to go there. It will take you a while to realize that you are looking at a much older map, and if you want to reach Delhi you need to look at a much newer map.

Similarly, if you looked at an older map to find the purpose of your mind, you probably wont find it. If it has too much unrealistic information far from reality, how will you find the right place in real life? Your context should be realistic and connected to the life you live right now. Only then you will find a meaningful purpose. In an unrealistic situation, you will find a purpose but that purpose will be closer to fakeness than reality. You might reach Uttarakhand instead of Delhi in that case.

My take from this method is to live life and be present for it. Be courageous to take part in things you love and be passionate about them. Help others to fulfil their purpose and find it and leave them in peace.

When you try this method, you will realize that the statement you wrote is similar and close to the reality you find yourself in: The reality you are aware of. For personal growth you need courage and that courage comes from passion. A good heart is important to feel loved by others or you love them. Unconditional love exists because we feel the need to feel connected to the things we like or are passionate about. Sometimes that passion is attached to other human beings. The feeling of growth and helping others grow is compassion, and compassion is the virtue of a good heart. You help others pursue the greater version of yourself; you make them feel conscious and aware of their situation when they need to know it; you help them figure out their purpose for growth. Leaving the world in peace does not mean to die. It means do not harm anything or anyone, improve life instead of degrading it and live your life with no regrets. Know that you did the best you could have done. You painted your heart out on those papers and you are satisfied now.

Method 2: Rational Intelligence

Apart from emotions, you have rationality. You can use reason and logic to find out the context of your purpose. The better you are at this the better your context will be.

In this method, you are fully aware of the reality and focus on it. You analyze your reality to find the context. The understanding of your reality tells you where you belong in reality. If you look at the rational side from a social context then you might not get a clear reason. Clarity is a much-needed quality. If you are hunting for a purpose in a social context, it is not possible. In the end, you will find yourself writing about your needs like earning more money, buying a car or getting out of the house loan. These are all need-based goals and you will be at round one again after accomplishing them. If someone else reads that statement, they will see the person they already know. There will be no newness in that.

I see life as an ongoing process of evolution. Every second, every minute of my life, I am evolving and turning into a better human being. This evolution is not of my biological form, it is an evolution of my personality. It is so simple to see it this way.

To some people, this approach is so simple that they almost miss it. They are searching for a context for their whole life and then living based on that. When you project your context on your life it becomes your purpose and the reality of your life.

If you imagine a hologram, you will see the whole figure. But if you cut a piece of it, that whole image will still be there; there will be no disturbance in its occurrence. Just like the hologram, reality is something big and you are only a part of it. You get to keep all the qualities of reality. That reality becomes you after a while and you start believing in it as much as you believe in yourself. If those beliefs are precise, the conclusion will be a realistic and sensible purpose.

This method is helpful because when you get a project, you can analyze it and see if it is a false belief that you were projecting on yourself. If that is true, then that purpose is wrong.

For example, if you believe that the Bhagavat Gitas beliefs are your reality, then your purpose will be to live by its teachings. In this case, you will live as the Gita teaches and spread its teachings.

If you have no reality whatsoever, then you will not have a purpose too. When you have nothing to project on yourself, you get nothing.

If you did not get a purpose that you like by this method, then you do not like the context you have. You need to resolve this conflict on your own. You can change the context if you like, but if you accept the context, you are accepting the purpose.

Blending the Two Methods

If you used both methods, you will end up with a purpose that you are excited about. You can also try this to see where it takes you. There are some hidden facts in your life that you ignore; using methods to bring them out makes you more aware of yourself. With emotional and rational methods, you will get two different purposes. Still, after going deeper in them you will realize they are the same and only you are looking at them differently. When you see two entirely different contexts, then your rationality and emotions are not compatible. Rationally, you are present in reality, but emotionally, you feel different. Maybe you read the Gita and believe in it as long as you feel good about it, but your whole life does not revolve around it. Your heart says it is what you should do but your mind says something else.

If you find yourself in this situation then try to figure out what is causing this conflict. Go through both parts and pick the right one. How will you know which one is right? See how you feel about what your mind has to say and then decide.

If your emotions tell you to paint but your mind says you should do something that helps people directly, you need to figure out what is in the middle of it. At what point do your emotions and mind speak the same way. Do not forget that your reality is your context. In this type of situation, there is normally an area that has not been cleared up yet: an area that is confusing and is in the middle of nowhere. This is why you probably never cleared it up. When you think about painting, a part of you feels that it is important to others too but the other part thinks there are so many things you can do in that time. When you stumble upon that uncleared area, you need a clear view to clear that and know what it is.

This process might become a little longer if there are several uncleared parts. For some of us, it requires proper cleaning in that fuzzy area with rationality to clear it.

It will take a different amount of time to clear those areas and get some clarity for each person.

MEANING OR JUST RANDOMNESS?

What would you call your existence – a random event or a purposeful plan? When a leaf blows in the air, do you believe that there is a purpose behind it? If we say that there is a power that does all this, then how does that power work? And if there is no power that does things physically, then it does not concern humans at all. If it doesnt concern humans, it also does not give any meaning to their lives.

Look at it this way. All humans are animals that evolved and became human. So before being humans they had no meaning in life because no one talks about the purpose of an animals life. So if other animals do not have a purpose assigned to them, why only humans? Do animals serve the purpose of being a humans food?

What makes human lives different? If god created humans, why did he only choose us to serve a purpose? Animals could have done that too. What was the process in which humans were attached to that purpose? Is this purpose something physical in the human body or it is found in the soul? How will someone find the true purpose that they were attached to at the time of creation? And if there is a meaning with every life, what was happening before one persons birth and what will happen after their death?

What does life mean? According to the dictionary, life is a state in which we are alive. When rockets with men were sent to the moon they were sent with the risk of getting some lives in danger or making big changes. At that time NASA gave a definition of life which includes everything that went through an evolution and is capable of converting energy.

Every life on earth mirrors the evolution of the process. On earth, it is about survival, the survival of the greater one based on the pleasure/pain principle. According to this principle, every living thing works under the impression of what is best for them – anything they can do to feel less pain and more pleasure. They believe others survival is painful for them to live and flourish.

This theory does not prove that every human works under the impression of what is best for them. It is in their genes that they do this, but when they are not working in that direction, they are self-destructing. People who are found self-destructive become a danger for others. And others, for their protection, cages them in so they can go on living like they always have. Being selfish is inbuilt in every creature. When we are working in our interest, we are living the life that is meant for us.

Evolution means "the survival of the fittest": how much one organism is capable of surviving in its changing environment and along with other organisms. If it did not have the inbuilt survival instinct, it will probably not survive. It will not replicate or evolve and its existence will get removed entirely from earth.

In this fight of survival, all living creatures fight each other for resources. Life forms such as bacteria or worms cannot control the environment around them. Humans are the only creatures that have evolved enough to use their minds. Humans are the only ones that can use their brain to use new ways of survival. They found security in their house while fighting for survival.

While surviving in the environment they built for themselves, only humans have developed enough to ask questions like why they are doing what they are doing? Only they can think about the purpose of their lives. No other animal is capable of thinking this way. Humans are so attached to purpose that they could end their life altogether by suicide if they do not find it. The real question then comes – to be or not to be?

TO BE OR NOT TO BE

Evolution has made us almost incapable of committing suicide. Our higher instinct of survival lessens our self-destructive qualities. When one does become self-destructive and commit suicide, they do it because they do not feel the energy within them to fight for survival anymore.

This survival mechanism embedded in our genes allows us to exist and cope with other organisms around us. This survival instinct forces us to keep making other humans so that the race can go on and never go extinct. The human race and other organisms exist on earth and evolve from time to time because they have survival instincts.

When the human race was evolving, they did not have the factual knowledge of reality around them, which is why they could not understand their environment better. If we want to survive and do better in our environment, we need to have factual knowledge. It is important to know the reality of things instead of just seeing them from a coated view.

Humans do everything they can to cope with the unexplained realities of life; they invented supernatural powers and people possessing them. They created god to believe in something, so they can have hope when everything seems to be dying out. They believed in prayers and sacrifices just to hope that their life will be better one day.

All these beliefs led to them believing that god created them and that god can control everything including what they do. These beliefs led them into thinking that they needed to please god to have a nice life, and their actions became according to their will. This all happened because humans needed to believe in something to be assured that they are safe and will survive no matter what.

There is no evidence that such supernatural beings exist. And if they do exist, there is no seeming proof that they affect any individuals life in any way, let alone give them a purpose to fulfil in their lives. If someone says that god is there to give people a purpose, then there are no written documents related to this subject. It could be a hollow belief or hallucination. These beliefs not only seem fake but they also contradict the evidence we have in actual life. Rational humans out there need rational proofs to believe such things, otherwise they are only empty words. If one believes in religion and its myths, they need to have faith in that religion.

American short-story writer Ambrose Bierce explained faith in a rather sharp tone. He said that believing in something without evidence is like believing someone saying something without knowing the subject. Anyone who believes in faith and destiny without any evidence chooses to avoid the factual evidence lying in front of them. They are scared to know the reality of things around them.

People who believe in unsupported evidence cannot face the environment in the right manner. This is what humans will have to suffer if they tried to find out the hidden god-built purpose in their life. This is a big price to pay to get satisfactory answers to their existence.

How is it possible that human life is attached with purpose either before or after its creation? When does god find a way to work on every individual? It only takes one egg and some sperm to create a human. What does god have to do with that?

Only eggs and sperm can make a human. It relies on two factors; one, which sperm will reach the egg first, and two, the sperm that reaches the egg is the most powerful sperm among several others and it will take its gene in the egg with it. And just like the survival of the fittest, the strongest sperm creates a human.

So based on facts there are only two factors associated with human creation. One, the survival of the fittest and two, random events. And if any other factors contribute to the creation either before or after the conception, they are not at work independently.

We have never encountered an event like this where creation is being manifested without any outer resources. Then it means there are no powers that affect an individuals life. This means there is no evidence that humans have an inbuilt purpose in their lives. Humans are nothing more than a random event and the survival of the sperm in the uterus.

It might not be satisfactory for some people that humans evolved and developed emotions and other skills, but there are no other proofs of anything else such as a purpose imposed in their lives.

A person who believes in god might say that humans were invented for a greater purpose and every human needs to do their part. But there is no evidence, not even a little to support this statement. Just because religious books say something, it does not mean it is true. People find it difficult to understand that they were born without meaning and have nothing to do in this world. It lowers their self-esteem and will to live.

Some philosophers find there is a lacking in human life if there is no purpose in it. This only pushes them to escape logic and reasoning. People who do not find any purpose in life feel that they need to find it themselves. They need to find the purpose and fulfil that to give meaning to life.

The escapists who escape from the truth create powers to believe in entities such as god and angels. They believe in them because they want to have a meaningful life.

If there is no purpose at all, then what should we do with our lives? It might not be motivating to see life as an empty vessel where evolution is the only thing that exists.

The truth is that human life and living in delusions of fancy powers are not the way to cope with reality. These delusions cannot change the fact. We need to stop being sad over our purposeless life and work on ourselves. We can use our time to enhance our living and be happy with what we have got.

Now we know that there is no superior being and we cannot also kill ourselves because of our survival instinct, so the only thing that can be done is to live life fully. We were not given a choice to exist or not when we were created, but we cannot try to escape from it by removing it from the face of the earth.

Instead of desperately trying to look for a purpose in our lives, lets try to live with the universal principle. We must survive and be happy and that happiness can be achieved by living a comfortable and painless life.

When there is no superior being we need to answer, we can live our lives by free will. We can choose where we fit in and how we want to see the world around us. You might not feel inspired enough to change the world or when you do, you might not change it in every way you want to, but now you have everything you desire in your hand... you have free will.

We can look at our lives and see something beautiful or we can look at something ugly. The universe does not care what we think about our lives so the only thing we can do is decide by ourselves and live by it.

One day we all shall die and this is how life works. We only get to live in the middle of birth and death. The randomness never leaves us, neither in life nor in death. A species cannot evolve if there are no deaths of its kind.

PERSPECTIVES ON HUMAN PURPOSE

People who do not have faith call rational view something in which there are no Gods or any supernatural powers. To them, having a rational view towards life does not bring you happiness just like believing in god does not. The difference between a system based on faith and a rational system is that in a rational system, people believe in the facts, they believe what they can see and experience. To them, if they have not seen god, then he is not there. Rationality is based on natural laws and science.

Saying that science is based on faith also shows a lack of knowledge of the subject and that is confusing. Science represents documents answering every question a person puts forth while believing in faith. Faith is true only for the person who chooses to ignore the facts presented by science. Science does not do miracles in life; in science, everything has a reason and everything repeats itself after a while. With science, you get precision and facts.

A scientific and rational view towards life sometimes shows some similarities between philosophical viewpoint towards life existentialism and scientific view.

Existentialism is nothing but a philosophy about the meaninglessness of life without a purpose. Existentialism also talks about how human beings should find their purpose and insert them within themselves. It talks about the purpose; it does not say why we need a purpose in life and why it is so important for us to live. Existentialism shows us the empty parts of our life which are not so empty for some people, it does not let us live life as it is and burdens us with its belief of purpose.

Religion and mythology try to show human existence as something having an external purpose, but it contradicts the evidence found in reality. Many people believe in the belief system non-supported by evidence. They find happiness in believing in a god who will favour them and make their lives bearable if only they keep praying.

Religion is the thing that creates guilt in peoples hearts; it is a fake sin which people are scared to commit. People get burdened by superstition and fake beliefs. Their beliefs force them to pray and ask for forgiveness for the sins they did not even commit. Living your life in such a way can bring joy and happiness but at what cost?

Humanism is another philosophy that talks about purpose. But in this philosophy, it does not talk about religion or myths; it only talks about how having a purpose improves the world and the condition of the people living in it. But this term has a loophole too; it doesnt tell us what it means by good or improved. If every individual believes in their concept of improvement, then Hitler too tried to make the world better in his way.

Further, humanists talk about the inbuilt dignity in humans. I do not think there is any concept of built-in dignity in people. Humans are a creation of evolution from a lower species of life. The humanist view towards life is not true because it only states the concepts of existence out of the evolutionary box.

When we accept the truth of life that our creation was random, we start living our lives without a burden of purpose or fulfilling our destiny. Evolution or emotions do not mean that life was given a purpose suddenly because humans started to use their brains and became emotionally developed.

If humans stopped believing in myths and supernatural powers and only focused on their happiness, half of the world would become happy in seconds. We associate our happiness with fake beliefs and wait for them to give us happiness. The important part of life is to find happiness on our own and not associating it with anyone or anything. We only waste our time when we think about absent sins.

Our happiness depends on anyone but ourselves; no one owes it to us to make us happy and we owe it to no one to make them happy. It is we who take it and lose it for our reasons. It is our loss if we surrender ourselves to someone elses hands to make ourselves happy. What makes us happy and what does not is entirely our own doing, so why is it associated with anyone else?

Theories that say we have a purpose to follow strip us of our happiness because we spend all our lives to find that purpose and fulfil it. We get scared that if that purpose does not get fulfilled, your life will be a waste. It also stops us from seeing the truth of our lives. If we found a purpose in life on our own, it will make us productive and deal with reality more comfortably.

Looking for a purpose in our life is equal to fakeness, because we let some beliefs stop us from dealing with our reality and environment in a better way. A view away from rationality will move us from living in an environment that is real and close. It changes the way we should live our lives. Instead of us deciding how we should live our lives, that purpose tells us how we should do it. Irrational views pull us away from success and happiness.

REVOLUTION

Some of you might have come to a concluding statement thinking this is what life is. But the truth is, this is not the end. There is more to life than just realizing something. You might think about what is going on and question if life is fake or real.

Existence does not depend on anyone. It is us whose thoughts and actions give meaning to our lives. For example, not everyone has experienced death, but we all know we will die one day. Similarly, we all believe that our life has meaning, only we need to decide what that meaning is. Only we decide what meaning we give to our lives. Here the search for purpose ends, but always observe instead of just seeing and always listen instead of just hearing. These rules can positively change anyones life.

Your mind can be trained in any manner you want to train it. You can either choose to make it a companion or a parasite. Our thoughts are limited to limited things. We create barriers in our minds. Open those barriers and let your mind wander from the most meaningful things to the most meaningless things. The results will only give you happiness because your mind does not feel restricted anymore. This process takes a while to be completed, but once it has been completed, you will become something new and find your old self miserable and depressing. It is like learning from your own mistakes.

Personal development is the best thing that an individual can do for oneself. And investing in oneself is better than investing anywhere else.

CONSCIOUS EVOLUTION

By evolution, I do not mean biological evolution in which organisms breed and mutate. To some people, this term might sound different and a little confusing. By evolution, I mean something greater than only biological changes. I mean the process which happens when one thing changes to come to a different stage that is more mature.

This evolution means growth in society, changes in thoughts, broader knowledge and a wider perspective on life. For example, we as humans have evolved and become like this in a thousand years, but it took only some years for humans to create technology and develop it every day.

So here the term evolution means the evolution of things created by humans. Biological evolution is much slower than other evolutions and it becomes irrelevant with time. If any changes occur in humans after some years or so, it will be only because humans participated in that process. It is not likely that evolution will happen on its own. The evolution which we all need right now is the evolution of other things outside of biology.

WHAT ABOUT THE BIOSPHERE, THOUGH?

Right now the environment is bad and we cannot wait for it to get better on its own; otherwise, the human race will become extinct entirely from the face of the earth. According to some environmental experts, the environment is so bad that we might not even get through this century. What we have done to earth cannot be reversed. We can only slow down the destruction and improve things.

Ignoring a problem does not solve the problem but starting a war against it suddenly will also fail to solve it. People are trying to attack the problem aggressively. They are making a little progress somehow, but I do not think they will ever reverse the situation. The decay is happening and will continue to happen without a proper approach. The resistance we see in the environment and pollution is too much; it might not be overcome for a long time.

If we take a little thing like diet into consideration, well see how bad its effect is on the environment. The American diet pollutes the environment and wastes resources, which is ignored by almost everyone. The government also ignores it because the food industry is so big. Compared to a vegan diet, a normal diet that a person takes when they are sad takes 18 times more land to cultivate food. If a person taking a sad diet took a vegan diet for a day, they will save as much water as they will save by not bathing for a year. Having a burger or pizza for dinner is not only a personal choice, but it also affects the environment. It does not matter what you do virtually, but if you are doing something in the physical world, it affects the environment no matter what you intended.

You can play an environmentalists role and become like Greenpeace, but that will only become a pretense after some time.

Some people are well aware of the consequences of their actions on the environment because of their knowledge of the subject. But still, they give in when marketers market their products. They eat everything and say it will help in sadness and depression. How is pizza supposed to make you feel better if you have just had an accident? Marketers do not mind if someone is cleaning a road or planting a tree, but when someone opposes the food that is supposed to harm the environment but makes them rich, then they will come at you to hunt you down. And they will do this till they get what they want.

There are so many things that harm the environment, and humans themselves create resistance when it comes to improving it. When people stumble upon content like this that talks about the harmful effects on the environment by humans, they will ignore it. People should have it in themselves to know what is going around. Only a small amount of people cares and try to do what they can to help the environment a little.

I think if we tried to solve the problem directly, it would not make any changes. Even if any of us tried to do something, we will be attacked by marketers whose business is getting affected by our movements. These marketers believe in the current system we live in and there is a possibility that some of them do not even care for the environment. If I tried to remove smoking from the society, I might get successful with some people but others will only ignore me. Where some will leave cigarette, others will start using it because there is so much going on with it. What I started will end in vain.

SO WHATS THE SOLUTION?

The solution is not direct and does not come into the role immediately, but it does help. What we can do best is to work on ourselves as human beings. We can help others to understand that it is important to grow as a person instead of growing as a money-making machine. Changes in the ways of our lives do not mean we need to make changes in our biology (it is not possible anyway); it only means that we need to do some change with our lifestyle and the way we think. We are evolved enough to do things that we are required to do. We only need discipline and courage to step out of our comfort zone and do whats right once in our lives. Many people only sit and think about various ways in which they can help but what they do is only think, and thinking does not bring any changes. On the other hand, I think that I can bring in a change and others seem to have the same conclusions too.

What time has taught me is that I can make changes within me by letting others with similar missions be around me. I am open to changes and growth and so are they.

Human beings are capable of so many things; they only need to realize their capabilities. The more realized people we have, the more strength we have. More of us will have the courage to step up. People will leave their destructive habits behind them and will adapt to new and improved habits. When they have a meaningful purpose in their lives, they will encourage others to find it too.

My mission is to encourage people to approach growth. I help them with their depression and instability of life. They find more courage and purpose to live after they have realized what life is worth and what they are worthy of.

I not only help others but this helps me too in my personal growth. My work on myself allows me to work on others. When I help others to gain full consciousness of their surroundings, I help myself too. I avoid the forces that scare me away from a conscious view of life and push me into a low conscious phase again.

The challenge that one sees while working on themselves is: how to live in the same environment they are continuously trying to change? Of course one cannot leave their job just because they need to find themselves. They need to stick to their jobs to fulfil their basic needs. To avoid bad situations, look for ways in which you can support yourself but do not have to invest much energy in it.

If you are conscious enough to understand your surroundings better, you can solve your problems without even attacking them. For example, if you know smoking kills and understand that, then you will not smoke at all and thus the smoking problem will solve itself. Personal growth can bring a positive effect on life.

Do not think that you are not investing more in the world. Only by personal growth, you can make changes in the world and you are not selfish to think about yourself. How are you supposed to make the world a better place when you are not in a good place?

STRAIGHTFORWARD

Some of us have a straightforward life. Such people do not worry about things and continue living as they have lived from the beginning. Their struggles have a pattern where everything fits perfectly and with time they overcome their problems. Sometimes they might find themselves being doubtful of things but it goes away too because their purpose keeps their mind at rest.

For others, life is not as straightforward. We find it difficult to even go through the whole day. Our troubles and anxiety strip us of our energy each day more and more. Even though we want to live, we do not find anything to live for. There is no positivity around us. And in this, illness or extra struggles gives a bonus to our troubles. For us, life is not fun, rather it is hard and we live with a heavy heart because we do not want to die.

So if you are a person who is looking for meaning in your life and want to know how to lessen the stress, then this book is for you. I will help you in finding a purpose and tell you how you can evaluate what you have achieved so far.

Very often, we all ask ourselves: Why am I here? What am I supposed to do now? And if you answered these questions without any trouble finding the answers, you are living a far better life than the rest of us. But if you could not answer these questions, then it is possible that you are not satisfied with the life you have right now. Our answers to these questions tell us what we think about our lives and where they are headed. It also forms our morals and beliefs. The real issue comes when we go out to look for the truth. How to find the truth? What is it? Without facts and truth, we cannot live our lives. Our beliefs and opinions will not matter if we do not know the truth. Is there any way to figure out the truth while we are still alive?

Are the things that are around us the truth? Is there anything else beyond the material? Does death bring an end to life or do we continue living after death but in a different world? Is there a god? And if there is, will we ever see him? And if there is one, why did he create evil and suffering? Why did god want humans to suffer? Why are there wars and killing even when people are only trying to worship their god? I wonder if all this even matters. There are thousands of questions in peoples minds but none of them ever get answered. Everyone is searching for the answers to their questions.

Some people do not even know that they are looking for answers. They spend all their lives in search of what they do not know. They often get to the wrong place and wonder if it was all worth it. This journey only pains them but it also pains others.

Everyone around us is suffering. We often look past their suffering and do not realize that they are almost like us, lost and confused. With drug abuse rising in every place, crimes are increasing too. Crimes have become more violent than ever before. There is sexual abuse at peak. Greed has become a part of human life and the word family means nothing to many. With time, humanity is sinking into darkness more and more. With corruption everywhere, humans are losing their have to have a grateful life. Without hope and purpose, there is not much to live for.

Humanity is falling in the pit day by day for no apparent reason. Humans always find something or the other to blame for their fall and plead themselves as victims. When we look at the old times, we realize that humanity was far better before than today. Our knowledge of ourselves and the world is greater than before, we should be grateful for evolving technology and everything that allows us to look deeper into things. But even after this, the human heart is darker and harder. They do not sympathize with each other; they have found greed and corruption to become their partner for life. Many things were considered a blessing before but is now a curse. The blessing has become a curse because the population and pollution have ruined the planet. Evil is increasing because history does not teach a human anything. They only listen to themselves and do not learn.

If this evil and darkness in the heart got replaced with love, then everything will be found. A dark place is where there is no light but with love, the heart finds the light. Why is there so much darkness and so less love? Why has humanity been ruined? Lets look for an answer to this.

IS THERE A CREATOR?

The first question which arises is how everything was created. Was there anyone who, one day, decided to make little humans and play with them? Because if he can control us, that means we are his puppets. From the beginning of time, people started believing in non-human beings whether it is a god or a ghost. They believed that God is a good person who takes care of them and ghosts are bad spirits that come from evil. In recent times, we also see other beliefs associated with ghosts such as a good soul that died and could not leave earth. I believe that nothing comes from just imagination; there has to be something that inspires a mind. Maybe those myths have some truth to them. If we compared old beliefs and events we will see that texts provide us with logical reason as to how and why humanity was created. For example, why was there a flood that drowned humankind and why were only some of them saved? Those texts and evidence have been corrupted and played with over time. Time played a great role in their existence and what they have become now.

The curious little human in us tells us to believe that there is a creator, otherwise, it does not make any sense. Without a creator or designer, things could not have been what they are now. And does it ask us to believe? Suppose there was an explosion around us and in that explosion, one mobile phone appears, unharmed even though it was in the middle of the explosion and working properly. Would you believe that that mobile phone has no purpose at all and it was saved for no reason? Would you believe that it has no purpose?

The first question that will come to your mind is: how did it get there and what are the materials that made that thing? You do not even know how that thing works and what its use is. The thing is, if something exists, someone must have created it. Otherwise, it cannot appear all of a sudden. When you have this in your mind, you will certainly look for a creator and ask him why he built that mobile phone and how to use it, its purpose, and if the creator has assigned it with a goal already?

Humans believe that the world was created with a big bang, but how is it possible for something to be created without any external power? There has to be something that triggered the existence of humans. If it was only a big bang, then there is no use of looking for an answer to why. But if it was not just a big bang, then why are we not getting answers? Science answers many questions but it does not clarify everything. If we look at the stars we know how they got there and why they are there. It also reveals how the earth and the entire solar system were created. But it does not answer our question.

If we go to science and try to figure out how such a complex life structure as our planet can be formed just by accident, we do not find any answers. If it was an accident, why are there no lives on other planets? Why are there no aliens and why do those planets not have lives like earths? When we could not find any answers, we started believing in magic, we started believing that it did start with a bang. Nothing answers the questions more clearly than the creator. Only a creator can create and form lives in such a manner; it cannot possibly be just an accident.

Biology and science have advanced so much with time that it is quite surprising if anyone does not believe in a creator. Both biology and science give us a deeper look into the creation of humans and earth. And the deeper we go the more we realize it cannot be just a coincidence. How can DNA be entirely different in each human being? Just a coincidence?

If we look at it scientifically, every other person cannot be inserted with new information. Science tells us that humans exist because of evolution but if that is so, then new information cannot be there only because of evolution. If one persons data got lost or misplaced, then there are chances of mutation, but mutation is not possible.

The human body works in so many amazing ways that it is hard not to believe in a creator. A human body is made of nerves and those nerves are connected to every body part. It cannot be a random incident. It is illogical if we believe that it is all science. Humans can never create what nature already has. It cannot create anything like a human being or an entire life system. It is a pattern and things have happened in that pattern. The first human was created and then he was left on earth to figure out how to survive by making his life more and more comfortable. Humans improved and made various things. They are improving more and more every day which we call modernization.

If god and ghosts are only beliefs, then science too only gives us theories. Darwins theory highly inspires these theories in *The Origin of Species*. The world accepted these theories because they had no other explanation, but in modern times, we see different things and those theories seem flawed.

The documentaries that we see nowadays only feed us myths. There is hardly any fact to them. But we accept those myths that science feeds us. Yes, we like mysteries and stories, but are they above truth?

If science is true, then it will not contradict the truth, but if it is incorrect, then it will.

We are humans and we are different from animals. Animals are not as evolved as us, hence they require no meaning. They do not want to know why they are here and what their purpose is. In a few words, life is a continuous journey of low and down paths and at the end of that journey lies death. So do we exist only to suffer and then die?

We spend half of our lives finding love and when we finally find it, we think *why were we looking for it?* When we are in love, we do not want it to ever end and if that is our purpose, then why do people suffer even after finding love? Why does one partner live longer than the other partner most of the time? Yes, death is a blessing to those who find life too hard to live, but what about those who love it and want to live longer?

The most contradictory part of a creator is death and suffering. Every religion talks about death and suffering but none of them clearly states why they are there. Why did god decide to give pain to his children? Suffering and pain put us in a dilemma whether god is loving or cruel. We deny believing in a creator that left us on our own and did not tell us why he created us. We have nothing to follow except for the wind that takes us nowhere. Adolf Hitler believed that he was working under the superior being, but all he did was bring sadness and cruelty into the world.

If there is no superior being, how do we have natural indicators of what is right and wrong? What about the laws of science? We continuously look for something better, something extraordinary and out of this world. And the satisfactory figure we find is god.

WHO IS THIS CREATOR?

Now we are almost convinced that there is a creator. But is it not possible that there are multiple creators? If we look at humans, we will see that every persons creation is not different. Everyone is similar but different from each other. If there are many creators, then from where did they appear? There has to be a source of them too. And if those creators created humans, then who created whom first and why? Some believe that it was aliens who created us and placed us here. If that is so, then where are they? It does not seem reliable. So in the end, we can only be convinced by the belief that god created humans.

There might be different definitions of god in different texts but everyone defines god as someone superior to us and who created us. This god has authority over all of us and everything. This is why there must be only one god. How can multiple Gods have authority over everything?

Now the question is, is god male or female? If god has a gender, then why has he/she not revealed themselves to humanity? Why does humanity not know if its a man for sure? In ancient texts, we see that god has been shown as a man. god is a spirit and does not contain a form; this is why it is not visible to humans. God has power over everything and he is the life force of all living things. We are a part of him and when we die, we combine with him again.

From the information we have of god, it is neither a female nor a male. It created both genders and attached them. There cannot be life formed without any one of these genders.

If there is a god and it has an identity, then it should reveal itself to humanity. From the theories we have read, human beings creation doesnt sound so soft and heart touching. It seems cruel and cold. Sometimes when there are too much chaos and disaster in the world, it feels like the world has lost control of things.

If god wants to reveal itself to us, it should be in front of several people to have more than one witness. Those people then can write about what it said and what it wants us to do. These manuscripts then can be read by everyone in future and present.

When god reveals itself, it needs to be visible to humans in a form they can understand. It should be in a way that humans can prove its existence to future generations. The best way to reveal itself is to be born as a human being and reveal then who it is.

THIS IS EXACTLY WHAT HE HAS DONE

God has always revealed himself as one among us. He establishes a kingdom (it does not need to be a kingdom; he gathers people and tries to bring them on the right path) and reveals himself among the people of his kingdom. Some of them believe him and some do not. They obey him and worship him but most importantly they believe in him and put their faith in him. From one part this revelation travels to another. That one part becomes a channel via which the entire world will know that there is a god in human form among them.

Previously, god has chosen to be on earth many times. He came as a prophet; he came as a king and sometimes came as a common human being. All these births of god were written by men in texts to know that there is a God. God has taken birth in every corner of the world to not be divided into various superior beings.

We try to look for the truth in our religious texts. In religious texts, there is hardly any question that goes unanswered. There is a theory for everything. Where some people put their entire faith in religious books, some do not. They criticize them and question them. I am not saying its wrong to question anything but it is just a little sad that our mind does not find peace anywhere. We cannot let disbeliefs and lack of faith move us from the search of truth. We must continue without any breaks. There are teachings of old religious books that get ignored many times. These teachings take us to the right path and help us in finding the truth. I believe one must look into these teachings with depth.

Sometimes you feel stuck and think that there can be no reason for you to be born. It is only a biological incident that you are born, otherwise, there is no other reason for your birth. Like grass, plants and animals, you too exist; like them, you too do not have meaning. The reason why we are here is so that we can continue forming more lives. If we stop, then the human race will cease to exist.

But if we are only a form of energy, why are we blessed with other things like the mind? Why have we been given the power of the mind that can create almost everything with the use of technology? How can he form new lives if we are only energies? Yes, it is true that one form of energy supports other forms of energies. Maybe this is the reason why we exist. But if humans did not exist, only one chain would have been lost, and other lives could have gone as they do right now. Cows eat grass and take energy from it; humans take energy from the cow, and worms take energy from a dead animal or humans body. This way energy passes from one being to another.

Our idea of looking for a meaning shows that we do have a meaning, otherwise we would have not been born. But what meaning could there be if we are only born to die? If death can be seen from life, it starts demeaning life. If life has value, then there is no death in sight.

When we host funerals we do not grieve for death, rather we celebrate life. We do not think about death because it torments us every second in life. When people ignore death and start living their life fully only then they can be truly happy. If death is in their mind all their life, they might be scared of taking risks and living because they are too scared of death.

If we had an aspiration or purpose then we might feel that our lives have meaning. This is truly our concept of living. When we are close to our goals or have achieved them, we realize that this is not for what the world will remember us. We will be forgotten with time and all our accomplishments will mean nothing when we die.

People say that it is best to do something that reminds other people of you. But my question is how long will they remember us? Our next-generation or the generation after that might remember us, but after that, we will be forgotten. The person who climbed Mount Everest or the person who stepped on the moon for the first time will always be remembered but other people like us who could not do something extraordinary like this will not be remembered till the end of time.

People think they have eternity to live for, but soon they realize eternity does not exist. A person can only live some years on earth; they cannot be there all the time. The general lifespan of a person is 70-80 years. Only some live past 80. Most of the people will be dead before 80.

I remember when an 80-year-old man I knew asked his doctor why he does not see people his age on the street anymore. The doctor said its because almost all of them are on their deathbed.

So why are we here? Why did we take birth if there is no meaning at all? Are we only alive to see our loved ones die and to wait for our own death too? Is there anything in our lives except for old memories?

We are intellectual beings and this is why we are sure there is a meaning to our existence. We know that it is not possible for us to be alive if there is no purpose whatsoever.

Our quest in life is to look for meaning. What nature and everybody tell us is that we have a purpose, but why do we not know what that purpose is? So it is up to us to find out what it is. At this point, I am sure we do not live only to die. You need to find the truth; you need to know why you are here. The meaning of life cannot be told to you by someone else even if they know it. You need to figure it out on your own. This is your journey to take.

In this quest of life, we sometimes see people who have their life figured out at such an early stage. It is refreshing to see them. Almost every human has complications in their lives. But some do not get affected much due to their privileged lives. But do those privileged people know the truth of life?

Those people who live their lives without getting affected by anything are not worried about their existence. They live their life daily, they sleep, wake up, eat, work and repeat. And in this process, their life goes by without affecting them or making them worried about their existence.

Man needs meaning to have a purpose. Without purpose, it is hard to live every day and not get tired of the same routine. What purpose will give satisfaction to a person depends on the person. For example, some people feel satisfied with religion and some do not. People who have faith in religion do not question things because their religion tells them everything. They have faith that every quest of life will be resolved.

SEEMS LIKE AN EASY WAY TO LIVE?

In faith, people mostly acknowledge what they know and leave the uncertainties of life to be answered by faith.

So when you have faith, is there any question left unanswered? Can everyone be a part of this quest or is it only for some individuals?

Does questioning things make you evil? When someone asks a question, they are stamped with the disbelievers tag or called unfaithful? Can we not have faith but at the same time have questions too?

To me, questions do not sound evil. They are the ones on which our modern society is based. Every religion is there to answer questions because there were people who asked questions and needed answers desperately before it. Questions founded faith in religion, but with time, people started neglecting questions. When they could not answer anymore, they called those people unfaithful. Many civilizations ignored the importance of questions and some started demonizing them.

Contemporary philosophers understood the importance of questions and they started inspiring other people too. But they had to wait for a long time for people to change and stand with them. Accomplishments like these cannot be achieved in the short term. It requires years and generations for some things to change.

When you ask a question and start looking for this answer, you develop reasoning, a theory to support what you have gathered. And when you have this information, you have a philosophy in your hand. People will not be affected by your theory for a while, but generations will spend their time thinking about what you said when you have strong reasoning. Philosophies take time to change others minds and finally live by those thoughts. Progress can only be made when there is a process going on and the first step is to think about human development.

Our relationship with God is nothing more than some rules set by other humans. Some human decided that there was God and he would have wanted us to live in a certain way, and we started believing in that.

The deep desire to have a meaning in life and have more clarity in life can be seen in the history of great minds. They posed questions and answered them themselves. They supported their answers with other peoples questions and answers. It has been this way for centuries.

Western philosophy is heavily influenced by Greek philosophers Aristotle and Plato. This Greek philosophy was taken into consideration while forming the eastern philosophy. Western philosophy then combined with Christian philosophy and became something greater. This combination of Greek and Christian philosophy was a huge step towards a new era.

The great philosopher Benedict de Spinozas philosophy was a huge controversy. He was excommunicated from his community and called an atheist. His philosophy may have been different from others but he was not an atheist. *Ethics* will prove that to you.

When he was alive, no one respected him as a philosopher, but he is now one of the most influential philosophers. Albert Einstein himself believed in "Spinozas God". He said, "I believe in Spinozas God who reveals Himself in the orderly harmony of what exists, not in a God who concerns himself with fates and actions of human beings."

Einstein believed in God but he never believed in a god that is personal. He believed that if we tried to understand God, we are trying to bring him to our level, which will degrade his status as a god. This is something Einstein never wanted to do and never did.

Einstein was someone who believed in questions. He looked for answers and presented them in front of us. His quest formed his personality and he became a man whom everyone liked.

Einstein defined life as:

Satisfaction of the desires and needs of all, as far as this can be achieved, and achievement of harmony and beauty in the human relationships. This presupposes a good deal of conscious thought and self-education.

It is undeniable that the enlightened Greeks and the old Oriental sages had achieved a higher level in this all-important field than what is alive in our schools and universities.

People live their lives in two ways. The first type of people is those who accept and believe everything that their religion has taught them. They have faith that no question will go unanswered. These people never question anything. They only accept what is given to them. Their belief and submission are so strong that only changes in religion can move them from one point to another.

These types of people are not happy with what they have received. They want to know more and look for more. They want to reach a higher reality. These people do not stick to the rules that humans made. They go beyond these rules and look for the truth. This is a group of non-religious people and highly religious people. In other words, people can belong to the first group but they might still not break the rule in the quest for truth.

When the Pope said that Limbo is not a genuine concept, millions of believers started agreeing with this statement. Before this statement, they would have fought with people who said that Limbo was not true. But now their beliefs were changed in seconds because the head of their religious group said it. It was almost like the whole religion was changed and people changed in seconds too. So, when you think your life is all figured out because you have faith in something, do not believe it.

Question everything you can and do not think you will be spoon-fed answers. Do not feel pain when you question something. Feel delighted to know why!

The race cannot be won without you running in it. Take your time to observe and finish the line of uncertainty.

FAITH-DRIVEN PURPOSE

If you had to define faith, how will you define it? I think faith is just an excuse so that people can rationalize fear. This fear comes from a superior being whom we do not even know. This fear of God drives us to do the right thing. Will you be at peace when you die? That depends on how much faith you have in God. A religion is formed around a deity and that deity is supposed to take care of us in our times of need. This God makes our life easy because it makes us fearless of other things. This superior being gives meaning to our life. With faith, life becomes meaningful. When you are a religious person, your purpose is to follow your religion because you have faith in your religion. Christian missionaries risk their lives to smuggle bibles into countries where they do not even know about Christianity, because they believe it is their purpose.

But when you no longer have faith in your religion, does your life become meaningless? How will you find your next goal then? Will you go look for another reason? The key is to look for a goal that is aside from anything. Some people believe that you can have a purpose only when you have faith, but that is not true. Faith is when you believe in something but there is no physical evidence of it. You only have faith because you can feel it. Faith is different for every other person. It is different in different countries too. People are fed different things at different places.

These missionaries believe tribespeople who live their lives without believing in any religion will be doomed. Their belief is that if someone does not believe in Christianity, then they will not go to heaven. If God was a saviour of other people and has shown himself to others, people might have believed in him. But that has not happened yet. Those tribespeople do have faith, but they do not need a God to have faith in something; they have faith in each other. Going out in the jungle fighting for life every day and winning food is the purpose of their lives. If someone told them that every one of their people would die soon, then they will do anything they can to spend every second of their life with them till they are around.

If you do not have faith in any religion or any deity, then do you have a purpose for life? Then the question arises if we have a purpose in life. Can there be any other reason for living other than following a religion and praying to God for safety?

Faith is not the same for everyone. Even a childs faith can be different from its parents. It means that faith did not exist on its own; man made it up. So if man made up faith then he can also decide his purpose. If someone does not have faith, then their purpose is driven by others who love them and whom they love. The purpose becomes only to be around them and taking care of them. It might not be someones conscious decision; it can be an unconscious decision too.

Faith gets stuck with doubt too when people ask if it is all worth it. If you do not have faith in God, then who do you have faith in? Humans? Humans kill each other every day and no one can do anything about it. How can you have faith in humans when you see them being so imperfect that they are ready to kill one of their own? We want control of our lives but the many times we lose is when we try to take it in our hands. What will your purpose be if there is no faith? Maybe you will never get an answer to this.

A BURNING CANDLE

Many questions have existed for centuries, but no one could give any satisfactory answers to them. Why are we here? What is our purpose? Why do we exist? People presented beautiful theories based on what they believe, but no answer was satisfactory enough. All these people set theories based on their past experiences or past reading. This is why there is nothing new to their stories. I think people never have anything new to think about. They read old stuff, see old people and then think about it. They form their ideas because they have seen some things. When they have seen or read enough, they combine those thoughts and put them together. This is when a person forms theories.

Nothing original can come from memories because your memories are old. And your brain cannot provide you with new ideas, only your existence can come up with originality.

Let us try to think about our lives for once. Let us put the idea of purpose aside for a while and see what this circle of life is in which we exist. We do things because we are able to think so and this becomes our routine to live. We think about things and then we do them. Both things do not happen the way we imagined or thought about. They always take their own turn. All philosophers talk about their ideas about life and what they believe is the right way to live. But how do they know if they are right? How do they know that those ideas are original or true?

When people ask saints and philosophers about the truth of life, most of them choose to stay quiet. They do not say anything because they cannot explain it or do not have an answer for it. But do these people have the answers? Do they know the truth? When these people are silent we try to understand their silence but will we ever understand it fully? We can try and try, but we might never be able to understand what that silence means.

When no one has the answer they say you can believe in anything you want to believe. Perhaps when a person chooses silence to treat a question, maybe they are trying to understand the circle of things themselves or say that they should have their own beliefs.

What is this circle? Have you ever found yourself in one? This circle is of those questions that other people get asked, and in answer to them, more questions arise. So when a person who has the answer hears these questions, they choose to stay quiet. With time questions like these become something bigger than one persons curiosity.

When people talk about a saint or a philosopher, they say he/she has reached the stage where they do not speak anymore. I believe their silence is not the absence of words but it is the absence of confusion from the mind. When one has understood everything, they do not need to explain it to others.

I think human life is similar to the life of a candle. Humans live and die every day like a candle and they live again. They are going towards their death eventually, but in this journey, they live and die so often that death does not matter. And even in this struggle, the wax of the candle stays even after its body dies.

When humans breathe, they live. When they let out their breath, they die. When they sleep they die, but when they wake up they live. Mystics believe that the whole universe dies every moment. This is why the universe feels so fresh and whole all the time. We do not have any proof for this but there is no actual proof for anything. We only have time that continues to pass no matter what happens.

I believe that it is true. I believe that we do die every moment. Otherwise, why would we make the same mistakes over and over? Why dont we feel tired of all the mistakes we did and try to do something different? Why do we torture ourselves when we know we will die in the end anyway?

The Sanskrit word Brahman suggests that a human cannot stop burning until there is a Brahman. He will burn like a candle and relive again and again. There will be death and there will be night and you will suffer pain. If you ever go beyond your mind, you will not feel tortured anymore, and the circle will end. When you are in the centre, you have no circle, but you cannot come in the middle if there is any confusion. Those circles which you see from the middle are the confusion of other humans. You do not participate in that confusion because you have stopped burning. You become the sun when you reach the stage of not burning. You are now an inspiration to others to follow your path and become a sun like you.

THE CLOUD

Just like clouds wander in the sky and form their shapes, humans can form their shapes too. Not always but sometimes you must have felt that you can have anything you want in life and can make your dreams come true. Life should be lived as a cloud. You should feel as light and as free as a cloud. It is not up to anyone to show you a path.

Everyone carves their path on their own. This book only gives you a hint about how you can carve your path, but following it is your own choice; no one can force you for that. Life is what you see it to be.

Decide your purpose in life and live by that. The desire to do something good and better will push you to choose a path if not today, then some other day, but it certainly will.

Made in the USA
Las Vegas, NV
15 February 2022

43965168R00046